Tweakings

and

Tappings

Tweakings and Tappings

When God Gets My Attention

Suzanne Jones

Cover Design by Elizabeth Jones

Published 2019 KDP

Dedication

There are so many people to thank for helping me with this project:

Janet, for putting the idea in my head to start with.

Heather Blanton, for giving me direction.

Heather Baker, for helping in *so many* ways.

Momma and Daddy, there isn't enough room to list all the reasons I have to thank you both.

Steve, for your support, love, and help.

My children, for helping me see things every day in a new light.

I love you all!

Table of Contents

Preface

I began writing these pieces a little over three years ago. The first one I wrote was "My Little Girl." I tried to write when I felt God was showing me something new or something I had missed, teaching me a lesson, or when a particular Scripture passage really stood out to me. Writing helped me to understand what I think He was trying to teach me. Most of these pieces involve my children in some way. I think God helps me see things through my children as much as through anyone or anything else.

These pieces are written in a very informal style, as if I am speaking. There are sentence fragments, but that is on purpose.

I hope that these little stories will make you smile, and perhaps stop and think.

Happy reading!

Suzanne Jones
July 2019

Hold My Hand

"Yet I am always with you; you hold me by my right hand."
Psalm 73:23 NIV

This evening my husband went outside with his binoculars to do some stargazing. It wasn't long before our three-year-old daughter was in dire need of her Daddy. Usually when he is outside and she wants him, she just runs right out the door, calling to him. She tried that tonight, but ran into a problem. It was dark.

So, back inside the house she came to get Mommy.

I walked out onto the carport with her. Her Daddy heard us and called to us from the end of the driveway. But she would have none of walking down the long, dark driveway by herself. Especially with the sound of the coyotes in the distance, howling down by the river.

Mommy had to go with her.

I took hold of her hand and we started down the dark driveway toward her Daddy. She was silent for a moment, and then said "I like it more better when it's light." I said to her "Elzie, I know you can't see, but I know where we're going. Hold tight to Mommy's hand."

We made it down the driveway, where she was reunited with Daddy. And everything was ok in her little world again.

As I walked back up the driveway to the house, I thought about what she said to me and what I said to her.

I, too, much prefer walking in the light.

It's easier when it's bright outside, there are no clouds (and no North Carolina summer humidity!) and the path is brightly lit. It's much harder when the way is dark.

Ever been there?

Things are dark. You can't see where you're going. You know where you want to go, but the way just isn't clear. And maybe there are "coyotes" in the distance, howling, making those steps in the dark seem even more foreboding.

What do you do in those times? What should we do?

Exactly what I told my daughter to do. Walk with Someone who knows where you're going. Hold *tightly* to His hand. Head toward the sound of your Father's voice, even if the voice is calling to you from the darkness.

This past year has been a dark one for me. There have been many good times, but there have also been plenty of dark times. Dark physically, dark emotionally. Dark. Dark. Dark.

One thing I *tried* to do during the darkest days was remember that God is in control. I didn't understand why some things happened the way they did. I still don't. I questioned Him. But I do know that He walked me through it. I know, *beyond the shadow of a doubt*, that He had hold of me during those times. Even when I didn't have the strength in myself to hold Him, He didn't let me go.

And there were the prayers of those who love me encouraging me to keep going. Put one foot in front of the other. Hold on, and keep going.

If times are dark now, hold tight. Listen to the sound of His voice. Head in that direction. Hold tightly.

If things are good, be the cheerleader from the sidelines. Send the card. Send the text. Most importantly, send a prayer.

And the coyotes? Don't forget that He made them, too. They also are subject to His authority. Ignore them. Like I told my little girl, they'll stop howling.

The Hidden Road

"Your road led through the sea, Your pathway through the mighty waters—a pathway no one knew was there!"
Psalm 77:19 NLT

My heart did a little jump when I heard the news. A jump for joy!

I quickly texted my husband to share the news with him. I got a response that said "I just saw. I'm offering a prayer of thanksgiving right now!"

I did the same.

What we were witnessing was an answer to our prayers. This wasn't something that was directly affecting us currently, but had in the past and unless something changed, would again in the future. Something we were not looking forward to having to deal with.

My husband and I had, in the past, discussed our course of action at length and had acted in what we felt was the best way we could. We had prayed about it. And then we had released it.

That was months ago. To be honest, this particular situation wasn't something I thought about all the time, or even for that matter, prayed about every day. Sure, there were days that I remembered to petition God for His hand to move, but I didn't do it daily.

I admit too, when I heard that our prayers had been answered, it startled me. I believe God hears us when we pray, I believe He answers us, but sometimes, ashamedly, I don't think I am *really* expecting the answer.

Pity.

God has shown Himself to be faithful, time and time again, in the stories we find in the Bible. I've seen Him handle things in my own life time after time. He has answered prayers in bigger and better ways than I could have imagined.

I wonder how many times God has thought about me the same thing He said to the disciples during the storm "Oh ye of little faith!" Why do I see His hand move again and again, and yet I still react the way I did this week to an answered prayer?

All this time, God had a plan, and things were moving in the direction that He had ordained. I, like the Israelites at the Red Sea, couldn't see where the path is going. Or, more accurately couldn't see the path at all. I couldn't see how the situation could resolve itself. I imagine I would have been like many of the Israelites facing the Red Sea with the Egyptian army bearing down on them from the rear. Wondering how this mess can be fixed.

But He sees. **He** knows. This Scripture from the Psalms confirms that *the path was there the whole time,* just unseen by human eyes. God knew it was there. He just had to move the water so the people could see.

The Scripture also tells us that the pathway led "through the mighty waters." They were indeed mighty waters, but the waters never touched the people of God. Didn't even get the hem of their garments muddy. Exodus 14:22 tells us that "The children of Israel went into the midst of the sea upon the **dry ground**: and the waters were a wall unto them on their right hand, and on their left." The mighty waters might have surrounded them, but on God's pathway they were safe.

I am sure that, daily, God works on that hidden pathway for me. I just need to have sense enough to trust Him, and continue to put one foot in the front of the other.

He knows and He is working.

I do believe Lord...help *my* unbelief.

And thank you, thank you, thank you Lord for moving in ways I cannot see and for handling yet another situation that I could not.

Loyalty

"Teach these new disciples to obey all the commands I have given you. And be sure of this: **I am with you always***, even to the end of the age."*
Matthew 28:20 NLT

We have had a case of the summer crud come through our house. First, it struck the youngest. She, who is never quiet, stayed on the loveseat for two days running a fever. She didn't want to do anything.

A couple of days after her fever stopped, her older brother began not acting like himself. Grumpy, nothing was right. He had gone to spend the night with the grandparents...just him, no little girls around (he is the only grandson of 5 grandchildren on my side of the family) but called to say he wanted to come home. I knew for sure and for certain then he was not feeling well.

So, onto the loveseat *he* went.

Mercifully for all of us, the bug was short lived with him, as it was with his sister.

The second night that he was sick and sleeping in the living room, I stepped out of our bedroom just before going to bed to check on him. Our dog was lying on the floor beside the loveseat, as close as he could get to it without actually being on it. Wide awake, head on his paws.

It was the sweetest looking sight.

Here is my little guy sick and asleep, and there is his (our) dog right beside him. Close as he could be. The dog looked as if he had settled in for the night right there beside his boy.

That is loyalty.

(And one of the many reasons I LOVE dogs!)

The dog was still there the next morning when I got up, in the very same spot, right beside his boy. It didn't look like he had moved all night. I imagined the dog looking at Jackson every now and then during the night, just to check on him. (I have no idea if that happened, but I like the mental picture.)

Dogs are loyal creatures. Loving and loyal. We have had many through the years, and those are traits that they have all shared. Unwavering loyalty and unconditional love. This one is no exception.

He is super excited to see us when we get home. He wants to be right there with us when we are outside. If the kids are on the swing set or the trampoline, he's right there too...just with them. Whether they are paying attention to him or not, he's there.

Dogs are more loyal than some people I know.

People will let you down, whether they mean to or not. Even people who love you. It's just impossible not to mess up at some point and let another person down.

But Jesus never will.

His parting words in Matthew are ones that I like to read when I am feeling bad, lonely, or just overwhelmed. He says that He is with me always.

Always.

Always.

When I am home, He is there. When I am in the car, He's there. When I am at church, He is there. He has promised never to leave me. He is the One I can always count on. Never will Jesus direct me to do something that isn't in my best interest. Never will He steer me wrong. Never will He stop loving me, wanting to spend time with me, or nudging me to come back to Him when I do something outside of His will.

"Even to the end of the age." That's pretty much from now until...forever.

There is nothing that can take Him from me. Nothing that can pull me from the safety of His hands. Romans 8:38 (another one of my "go to" verses) puts it this way: "And I am convinced that nothing can ever separate us from God's love. Neither death nor life, neither angels nor demons, neither our fears for today nor our worries about tomorrow—not even the powers of hell can separate us from God's love."

Those are some super promises in those two verses. God's love, Christ's love, is constant, sure, and strong. Nothing can separate us from Him. He promises to be with us/me forever. His presence is always with me, and He's always ready to listen, advise, direct, and love.

And He never takes time away from me to chase the deer.

Master Tailor

"The Lord God made garments of skin for Adam and his wife and clothed them."
Genesis 3:21 NIV

A few years ago my friend Janet asked me if I would be interested in making a Jesse tree with some other people. Another friend of ours was putting together a Jesse tree ornament exchange and Janet (who is WAY more creative than I am) had seen it and thought I might enjoy participating with my kids.

I had never heard of a Jesse tree, but after looking it up, decided to give it a shot.

I am not artistic at all and the ornaments my son and I made reflect that. Very basic. But, some of the ornaments made by other people are really impressive. We've got a crown of gold, a stitched coat of many colors, and a cluster of grapes just to name a few.

The nightly Jesse tree reading and ornament placing has become a favorite Christmas tradition with my kids. Most nights the question "Is it my night to hang the ornament?" comes from at least one of them before we begin.

Tonight, the reading was taken from Genesis 3. We read from verse 1 all the way through verse 21. This is the story of Satan tempting Eve to eat the fruit of the tree of knowledge of good and evil and the subsequent punishment from God for their disobedience. Familiar reading, but tonight I noticed something I had never noticed before in verse 21.

"The Lord God made garments of skin for Adam and his wife and clothed them."

What I noticed for the first time was Who made the garments.

The Lord God.

Even in the midst of doling out punishment, God was merciful and saw fit to do something to make the punishment bearable.

I had always focused on the punishment up until tonight.

But here we have, I think, the first example of God showing that His mercy extends even through His punishment. Adam and Eve had just been expelled from the Garden of Eden. Kicked out of the only place they had ever known. Destined now to work for everything they had. Experience the pain of childbirth. And they were ashamed.

So, what did God do?

He made clothes for them, and then He Himself clothed them.

The Scripture tells us that "God made garments" for Adam and Eve. I don't know, but I can imagine that the garments the Lord made for them were far superior to the fig leaf clothes they had sewn together.

But the bigger point in my mind is that God didn't just punish them, kick them out, and leave them. He still provided for them. He still took care of them. He still took time and *did something* to ease their discomfort. He didn't just leave it up to them to do the best they could. He did not just leave them with their mess and say "Good luck." He helped. Even in their disobedience, He was there.

That reminds me that even when I feel the discipline of God, not to lose heart. Proverbs 3:12 tells us "The Lord disciplines those He loves." His discipline is to correct us, help us, and bring us closer to Him.

It also reminds me that even when I have made a mess of things and I am dealing with the consequences of my behavior, God is there to provide.

To provide in ways that I can't.

To "sew up" my mess and clothe me.

To care for me, even in my disobedience.

Even in their punishment, God never left Adam and Eve, or abandoned them. Just as Jesus promised in the New Testament that He wouldn't.

I am grateful that God loves me enough to discipline me (even though it hurts) and merciful enough to help me through it.

Tent Prayers

"But Jesus said, 'Let the children come to me. Don't stop them! For the Kingdom of Heaven belongs to those who are like these children.'"
Matthew 19:14 NLT

One afternoon not too long ago while we were in the living room, my three-year-old daughter made an out of the blue announcement. "I want 12 more babies! Ten boys and 2 girls!" Before I could say anything, she said "I'm gonna pray about it!" and hopped off the loveseat into the tent made of bedsheets and chairs the kids had been playing in and prayed. In very simple words, and with a great deal of sincerity, she said "Dear God, I want 12 more babies. Ten boys and 2 girls. Amen."

And that was it. She jumped up and was on to the next thing.

I am 42, have a son and a daughter, and last year had two miscarriages in 7 months, both after normal ultrasounds. The resulting surgery from the last one landed me in the ER with an overnight stay in the hospital.

It will take the hand of God moving for me to have another child.

But that is not what struck me about Elizabeth's prayer.

There were other things.

The first was that her first step, her first course of action was to pray. She didn't talk to anyone else (including her mother!), she talked to God. Now, she is just three and her circle is a *tad bit* limited, but, she spoke first to God about her desires. I do not mean to say that we shouldn't talk to our Godly friends and family. I believe we should. I believe that God puts these people in our lives for reasons. He speaks through them many times. But they should not be the first, or the only, place we turn. I am grateful for the Godly men and women that He has put in my life. They have been, and continue to be, a source of comfort, wisdom and inspiration for me. But God should still be the first one I speak to.

Another thing that struck me about her prayer was the simplicity of it. No fancy words, no begging, no pleading, no bargaining, no cajoling, just her request. Just her desire. In plain and simple words, laid out before the One Who can do something about it.

I wonder sometimes why I don't do that more often. Just talk to Him the way I talk to my best friends. Sometimes a quick text to or from one of them speaks volumes. And a quick word or moment with Him can make a huge difference, too.

Again, I know my daughter's prayers are simpler because she is so young. But she said what she needed to say. That was it.

Of course, my friends and I wouldn't have the relationships we have if we hadn't spent time together and if we didn't have in-depth, long conversations, but we don't have to do that *all the time*. Same way with the Lord. Each time we speak, it doesn't have to be big fancy five dollar words that take 30 minutes to say.

The other thing that stuck with me was that after she presented her request to God, she got up and moved on. She didn't get back up and moan and groan about it. She didn't get up and mope. She got up, and moved on. She took her request to Him and left it with Him.

All this to say that the way she prayed, and the attitude with which she prayed, made me stop and think, and re-examine my prayer life. I think I could take a lesson from my little one...take everything to Him, take it to Him first, and leave it with Him.

The faith of a child.

Thanks, Elzie.

Saturday

"The women were terrified and bowed with their faces to the ground. Then the men asked, 'Why are you looking among the dead for someone who is alive? He isn't here! He is risen from the dead!'"
Luke 24:5-6 NLT

One of our Easter traditions is reading Passion Week Scripture. Each day from Palm Sunday through Easter Sunday we read the account of what Jesus was doing some 2,000 years ago at this time. Today being Saturday, there wasn't as much reading as there was for yesterday, Good Friday.

The short reading for today was about the burial of Jesus (John 19:38-42).

When my tweenager commented on the smaller amount of reading today, my husband reminded him that the day between the crucifixion and the resurrection was the Jewish Sabbath and work was not allowed.

So, the question from the kids was then "What did they do?" ("They" being the followers of Jesus.)

Good question.

I don't know that I had ever given much thought to what they did on Saturday. I guess because I know the "rest of the story." I know how it ends and I tend to skip over Saturday, right to the "good stuff" on Sunday. We know that Sunday morning will bring wonders beyond wonders and hope where hope had fled. We know that Sunday will bring an empty tomb.

They didn't.

Or at least they had forgotten.

I think I know what I would have been doing if I had been there. The same thing I do now when something overwhelming happens.

Sitting somewhere in the dark, trying to process what just happened to my world.

Sometimes for me when something really bad happens, especially something unexpected, the days following the event are harder than the day that it happened. That's when it starts to sink in, when the chaos turns to quiet and I have time to think about what happened.

To be sure the events of the past week had seemed surreal to the women and the disciples. How did the situation go from Jesus riding into Jerusalem being cheered to Him dying a horrific criminal's death?

How did things go from Jesus healing the sick, the lame, and the blind to being tortured and killed Himself?

It *had* to be hard to process.

What a dark day that must have been. What feelings of hopelessness I can imagine they felt.

They didn't know what we know.

Saturday is dark, but Sunday won't be.

On Saturday it seemed the Light of the World had been extinguished. On Sunday, the Light would come bursting forth!

The time of their deepest, darkest sadness was about to give way to their most joyous, unbelievable day!

What is the lesson for me in this?

Sometimes the things that happen in life knock you down. Waaaayyyy down. Hard. Fast. The situations are too big to handle. But God has got something planned. I may not see the plan, I may not have *any* concept of how He is going to handle things, but He does. He **is** going to handle it. He **is** going to take care of things. And He **is** going to carry me through.

Just as for the women in the Scripture at the tomb, things might be about to turn around in a BIG way!

I think the words from the Phillips, Craig and Dean song "Little Bit of Morning" sum it up pretty well: "Though the darkness for a moment, May hide tomorrow's light, Just beyond what the eyes can see, The light of hope is bright."

The Hope the angels announced that day is the Hope we still have today. "Why do you seek the Living among the dead? HE IS NOT HERE! HE IS RISEN!!"

AMEN AND AMEN.

Seeing the Sea Serpent

"So I concluded there is nothing better than to be happy and enjoy ourselves as long as we can."
Ecclesiastes 3:12 NLT

Some time ago I saw a post on someone's Facebook page that went something like this: "Lionel Richie never had to get children ready for church on Sunday morning" in reference to his song "Easy Like Sunday Morning." Sometimes Sunday mornings are super hectic, getting everyone cleaned up, dressed in their Sunday clothes, and out the door in time to make it to opening assembly.

The kids and I had just slid into the back pew one Sunday a few weeks ago, before the service started. And as usual, they were both talking, both moving and both vying for my attention. Elizabeth was trying to get her little pocketbook in just the right spot, and my help was apparently necessary to move it from place to place. Jackson was trying to show me something he had drawn on the bulletin in the nanosecond that we had been there. I was trying to get my things situated in the pew and take a brief glance at the bulletin before the opening prayer.

As I sat Elizabeth's pocketbook out of my way for the umpteenth time, again, trying to look at the bulletin to make sure I wasn't supposed to be somewhere that morning, Jackson said "Momma! Look!"

I glanced briefly at the bulletin not really looking at the image, or making an effort to see it and said "Yeah, that's nice."

My ten-year-old stopped, looked at me and said "Well, I can tell you don't really care about that!"

Boom.

That took the wind right out of my sail. Pretty sure I'm in the running for the Mother of the Year award there. May have it locked up.

His comment made me take a look at myself in that moment, and a look at myself in other moments, too. I do care about what he does. I care about what he does with his free time, what he does in school, what he watches on

TV, what he reads. Why? Because he is my son, my first born, and I love him. More than life itself.

But there are times when I haven't given him my full attention when he calls "Momma!" like at church a few weeks ago. Usually it is because I am behind in doing the things I have on my checklist for that day. Sometimes that can't be helped. Supper has to be cooked. His lunch has to be packed. We do need clean clothes. And sometimes Momma does need a few minutes of quiet! But there are times I could stop what I'm doing and enjoy a moment with him.

The scripture from Ecclesiastes reminds us to be happy and to enjoy ourselves "as long as we can." Sometimes that means taking a step back from the things that I feel like *have* to be done to just enjoy the blessings He has given me, and enjoy the blessing *in the moment.*

Take a few extra minutes outside and play with my dog who is always so excited when we get home. Turn the radio up a little bit louder and enjoy that long lost 80's song. Take the time to push the laundry folding aside and watch my son jump to try to touch the ceiling again. Stop typing the email for just a second and bite the head off a gummy bear with my little guy. (Do little girls do this, or just boys?)

Take the time to be grateful that at least for the moment, before the teenage years hit, he wants to be with me.

Wants to talk to me. Wants to show me the sea serpent that he drew on the church bulletin.

And be grateful that our Father in heaven is never, never too busy to listen to me. Anytime, anywhere, and for any reason. That right there is cause for happiness!

Contentment

"I am not saying this because I am in need, for I have learned to be content whatever the circumstances."
Philippians 4:11 NIV

Sitting on the couch nursing a 102 degree fever was not how I had planned to spend this Saturday night.

Nope. Not at all.

This was supposed to be the night that my hubby and I went out to supper with some of our friends as a Christmas present from one of those friends.

Not just to Cracker Barrel or Golden Corral - although I love them both. This night was a "get dressed up in your finest and leave the kids at home" kind of night.

It is one of the evenings I most look forward to during the year. The restaurant is a *fine dining* establishment. The kind that serves everyone's plate all at once, everyone having a separate server to set the food down at exactly the same moment. The presentation is beautiful and the food tastes exquisite. (I am not sure I even know what half of the menu items are. Suffice it to say, there are no French fries.) The company is fantastic. The conversations are always fun. And my husband looks amazing in his suit which accentuates his broad shoulders.

But it was not to be tonight.

Even if I had felt well enough to go, the flu diagnosis from the day before would have prevented it.

So, change of plans.

But, as I sat on the couch looking around at things, an unexpected feeling began to settle over me.

I think I would call it "contentment."

Now, I was not at all content with being sick. But contentment with life in general.

I sat on my comfy couch with my Civil War book in hand. Surrounding me were pictures of my family...a picture of my son in his baseball uniform with his sister kicking her leg up in the background. Our Christmas pictures hung on the wall. On the side table and bookcase there are now two pictures from my parents' wedding (two of my favorite Christmas gifts this year). One picture shows my Mom and Dad with both sets of my grandparents. The other picture shows Mom and Dad and my 4 great-grandparents who were still here at Momma and Daddy's wedding. I knew all but my Daddy's grandparents who passed away in the three years between Momma and Daddy's wedding and my birth.

There's a picture of my now "tweenage" son as a 2 year old. There's a picture of four generations of the Brown family: my Papa, my Momma, my son and me. There's a picture of my brother and me as small children with our grandparents. And there are pictures of members of my husband's family that I never had the chance to meet.

Our living room may not be very neat and clean, but it has a warm and homey feeling.

My husband was in the next room with his book, trying to catch a moment of quiet from having to be Mommy, Daddy and Nurse for the past couple of days. Our son was reading as well, on the loveseat next to me. Our daughter, never one for being still or quiet, was back and forth between her brother and father while playing with various toys in the living room.

It felt good.

I didn't feel good, but *life* felt good. Being surrounded by people I love and by memories of people I loved.

I think for a *brief* moment, I caught an understanding of what Paul meant when he said he had learned to be content whatever the circumstances. This is certainly not something I have mastered, but I think it came through a bit Saturday night.

Being content with where I was in life and where I was for the evening. Being content with what, and with whom, God has blessed me. Blessed me despite myself.

I am glad God nudged me Saturday night. Even if He had to send the flu to get my attention.

Then Jesus Wept

"Then Jesus wept."
John 11:35 NIV

I had spent the day with my daughter, my parents, my sister-in-law and my two youngest nieces at a local park. It was a beautiful September day in North Carolina, still plenty warm, but not scorching, with relatively low humidity. We rode the merry-go-round, played in the sand, went down the slide and rode the train. Several times. The little girls (all ages three and under) had a grand time.

Top that all off with a trip to Chick-fil-A. What more could someone want?

But I had been dreading the day for weeks.

Not the time with my family, or the park, or even the fast food.

The date.

September 14.

My due date.

Or, it was my due date.

But in March, we lost this baby. The second one in 7 months. Both after ultrasounds where we had seen the baby and heard the heartbeat. The first of these losses was around week 10. This second one was in the second trimester - after two ultrasounds - neither with any signs or symptoms that anything was wrong. The subsequent surgery the second time was hard on my body, leaving me with a nasty infection that landed me in the emergency room a week later, and then an overnight stay in the hospital. Follow that with lots of heavy antibiotics, which had a host of *really nasty* side effects.

The physical portion of the ordeal healed pretty quickly.

The emotional part, well...not as quickly.

Gradually things did get better for me. I didn't think about the baby every day. Eventually, things got back to our normal. Church activities, baseball, summer vacation. And then, the start of school for my older child.

Late in the summer I sat down with my son's school calendar to put all the important events on my own calendar. When I turned the page from August, there it was.

September.

I had been conveniently ignoring the existence of the month. But there it was, staring at me from the pages of my calendar.

As much as I tried during the first part of the month to forget what was supposed to happen, the closer the date got, the harder it got. And the gloomier I became.

Until the official day.

I tried very hard to put on a happy face for my daughter and my nieces, but by the time I got home that afternoon, I was exhausted. I found that I was having trouble holding back the tears. And I felt guilty. Guilty for crying when I have two healthy, happy children. Guilty for being weepy around the kids. Guilty for feeling sad. Guilty for not being "strong enough."

As I sat at my son's guitar lesson that night, I got to thinking about feeling guilty and weak. Then I remembered the scripture from John, when Jesus arrives at the tomb of his friend Lazarus, "And Jesus wept." *Jesus* wept. The *Creator* wept. He who was able to do something about death, (**and did**), cried.

I have thought about that a lot since then.

It has always been hard for me to wrap my head around Jesus being fully human and fully God, but He was. We live in a broken world, in broken bodies, that sometimes betray us. Jesus, being fully human, experienced that too. He experienced grief. He cried. He loved, and He cried.

If Christ, who holds the keys to life and death, allowed Himself to cry when He hurt, what is wrong with me crying when I am grieving? And you know what I think the answer is?

Nothing.

There is nothing wrong with crying when you hurt. There is nothing wrong with feeling the disappointment, the loss, the broken dreams, and crying about it. We're *human*, not *superhuman*, and we are not home yet. We live in an imperfect place, in imperfect bodies, and sometimes it hurts.

But I think the key is in continuing to read the story. Jesus cried, but then later in verse 41, scripture tells us that Jesus looked up, and spoke to His Father. We have to look up.

We have to look to Him for our strength, our Peace, and our Comfort. If we continue to look at our situation, sometimes it seems hopeless. We have to look up, look to Him.

Jesus assures us that He is the Resurrection and the Life (John 11:25). All who believe in Him will spend eternity with Him. I believe that on the day I see Him in heaven I will be able to hold my children that I never held on earth.

Until then...Mommy loves you all.

Lessons from a Bad Hair Day

"Don't be concerned about the outward beauty of fancy hairstyles, expensive jewelry, or beautiful clothes. You should clothe yourselves instead with the beauty that comes from within, the unfading beauty of a gentle and quiet spirit, which is so precious to God."
1 Peter 3:3-4 NLT

This past week I took my four-year-old daughter to get a summer haircut. Since it is so hot right now (100 degrees in NC with some pretty high humidity), I thought I would get a trim too (although I wasn't at my normal "hair place"). Thinking that a shorter cut would look nice on both of us for the summer, I went for shorter than we have had in a while.

My daughter has stick-straight, fine hair. Her shorter summer cut looks great.

Mine. Does. Not.

In fact, I hate it.

Not sure why I do this over and over again. My hair is thick. Coarse. Full of what during the less humid times of the year is body but during the summer is kink and frizz. Every time I cut my hair shorter, I hate it. Don't know why I thought this one would be any different.

I look like a mushroom.

But thankfully, my hair grows quickly.

After I moaned to my husband about how bad my hair looks, I thought about beauty and ugliness and our perception of each. I have heard my grandmother say many times, "Beauty is only skin deep, but ugly goes clear to the bone!" Of course she meant that someone can be nice to look at on the outside while being totally rotten inside.

I've known some people like that.

And I've known people who became more attractive the more time I spent around them. All because of their attitude and personality.

The scripture from 1 Peter tells us that true beauty does come from within, from "a gentle and quiet spirit."

That has *not* applied to me over the last couple of days.

With 100 degree heat and about that much humidity, we have sheltered in the air conditioning. Not so bad for a little while but it is not the best way for active children to spend the day. My patience and the temperature have had an inverse relationship...as the thermometer has crept up, my temper fuse has gotten shorter. My patience level has dipped to record lows and I'm pretty sure my decibel level has risen to record highs.

Probably not the best example of a "gentle" or "quiet" spirit.

Lately I think if my outer beauty had been a reflection of my inner beauty I would have looked like some freakish cross between Shrek and Frankenstein.

Not pretty at all.

Raising my voice at my kids is not a gentle spirit. Snapping at my husband is not a quiet spirit. Muttering under my breath hardly qualifies.

We all get tired from life...even when life is good, it can still be tiring. The lesson for me is not to let the little frustrations turn into a big attitude problem. Concentrate on being gentle...being calm. On not letting the redhead in me rear its mushroom-haired head.

The nice part about this type of calm inner beauty is that it is "unfading." Age doesn't affect it. Too much sun doesn't affect it. It doesn't gray, it doesn't sag, and it doesn't cease to fit the way it used to. Just as beautiful year after year. Unfading.

Mercifully, this haircut does not follow suit.

Good Gifts

"So if you sinful people know how to give good gifts to your children, how much more will your heavenly Father give the Holy Spirit to those who ask him."
Luke 11:13 NLT

I woke up first on Christmas morning. Looked at the clock. Tried to sleep some more. Couldn't.

So, I got up. "Everyone else will be up soon" I thought to myself.

I took my shower. Still no one up, although my husband was starting to stir.

Headed to the kitchen. Fixed my coffee.

Still all quiet in the rest of the house.

Read my Bible.

Now Steve was up, but no children.

By this point, it was all I could do not to wake them all up.

I think I am more excited about Christmas presents as a parent than I was as a child.

As the Mom of the family, I know *most* of what is under the tree. And I want the rest of the family to see.

I want to go into their bedrooms and wake them.

Jackson!! Jackson!! Wake up!!! Don't you know what we put under the tree??? It's the present you've been asking us to buy for at least 2 months. And the Houston Astros jersey you wanted...it's in there too!! And the next movie in The Hobbit trilogy...it's under the tree! Wake up!! Wake up!!

Elizabeth!! Elizabeth!! Wake up!!! Don't you want to see the pink bike that Santa left for you??? There is a place on the back for you to put one of your baby dolls. There's a Play-Doh fun factory in there. You'll love it! And a Donald Duck doll and a Goofy doll under the tree. Wake up!! Wake up!!

But I sit and wait.

And it is worth it. Once they are all up, the excitement of Christmas morning is something to be remembered and relished.

This year, Christmas is on a Sunday. So after we checked in with Santa, we had a quick breakfast and headed to church.

As I sat in the pew with my children and my son's friend, I couldn't help but think of how excited I had been this morning and how ready to get things rolling I was.

And I wondered to myself "Is this how God felt on the first Christmas all those years ago?"

Wake up World, wake up! Don't you know what has just happened? Don't you want to see this amazing Gift I have just given to you? Wait until you see...wait until you hear...wait until you experience the joy of My Christmas gift. Salvation has been born! I've sent you the King of Kings and Lord of Lords! Wake up!! Wake up!!

Was God just as excited to "get things rolling" as I was? Did he want to shake the sleeping world awake so that the Gift could be realized? So that the Gift could be enjoyed? So that we could see a glimpse of how much He loves us?

I like to think that He was.

Luke 11:13 tells us this: "So if you sinful people know how to give good gifts to your children, how much more will your heavenly Father give the Holy Spirit to those who ask him."

And I think God is happy to give us the Holy Spirit. I think He was excited to send us His Son. Even knowing what would happen to Him, even knowing that He would be rejected by some and ridiculed by others, He would be the Light to some. And He would be the Light for ages to come, for countless generations.

He would love the unlovable.

He would give hope to the hopeless.

Sight to the blind.

Movement to the lame.

Life to the dead.

And life everlasting to those who call Him "Savior and King."

Our Christmas tree was overflowing with gifts this year. Given to those we love because we love them.

And 2,000 years ago the love of God overflowed from heaven, to a tiny town, to what was probably no more than a small cave, in the form of a tiny baby.

One of the Christmas cards we got this year summed it up well: "Only God could put a love so great, in such a small package."

Thank you God for the most perfect Christmas present of all!

Homecoming

"So the people went away to eat and drink at a festive meal, to share gifts of food, and to celebrate with great joy because they had heard God's words and understood them."
Nehemiah 8:12 NLT

I have been to three church Homecomings in three weeks. That is three weeks of catching up with old friends, meeting new additions to families, and three weeks of *really* good food.

Each place I went holds a special place in my heart. The first Homecoming service was the church where my father is currently the pastor. I never attended there as a member since Daddy was called there long after I was grown and living on my own. This is Daddy's home church. I went with my grandparents as a child. They are buried there. As are several earlier generations of my ancestors.

There are some super people here. And some really good cooks.

The second homecoming is the church to which my husband and I belong, which happens to be my husband's home church; the one he grew up in and has remained active in as an adult. It's right down the road from our house. And the folks here have opened their arms to me and welcomed me. I've made many good friends and look forward to Sunday mornings. Homecoming here always involves eating under the grove of trees (weather permitting) and then a walk through the cemetery where my husband and a couple of friends tell stories about many of the people buried here that I never got the chance to know.

Great people here. And there are some really good cooks.

The third church in my Homecoming tour was one my father pastored as I was finishing high school and heading off to college. So many good people there. I learned to make pimiento cheese from the pimiento cheese master who went to church here. And the world's best fried squash can be found here.

Good memories in all three places.

In just a few weeks, I get to go to Homecoming at my home church. More good food, family and great friends I don't get to see nearly enough.

I think it is important to go.

It is good to reconnect. It is good to be with other Christians and to worship together. In fact it is necessary. I know on Sundays when I am unable to go to church, if I'm sick, or I'm home with a sick child, my week feels off.

We see example after example in the Bible of believers gathering together. Being with like-minded people is an encouragement to us. A way to stay on the straight and narrow.

We're even told in Hebrews that we *should* get together. The author tells us "And let us not neglect our meeting together, as some people do, but encourage one another, especially now that the day of His return is drawing near." (Hebrews 10:25 NLT)

Encouraging one another. It makes a difference to have the support of people who believe as you do. Often times at our Southern Baptist Church our gatherings involve food. Each of the Homecoming services ended just as the verses in Nehemiah said...we celebrated with great joy because we had heard God's Word. We shared the gift of food. All the meals are pot-luck...so everyone brings something to share.

The food is shared, the time is shared and the memories are shared.

Next year, the memories from this year will be shared.

And one day, we will take part in the greatest Homecoming celebration imaginable. We will see again all the friends and family that left this earth before us. I'll get to spend time with my grandparents, with some friends who died too young, and with my babies I never held in my arms, only in my heart. And even better than all that, we will eat with The King. The One who made it possible to enjoy such a Homecoming instead of getting what our sins declare we should...eternity without Him. What a homecoming that must be...something He has prepared for us...for US...His children.

I wonder if they have sweet tea and banana pudding in heaven...

My Little Girl

"Greater love has no one than this: to lay down one's life for one's friends."
John 15:13 NIV

This week has been busy so far. Many preparations to make. And every now and then I have to stop to cry.

My 3-year-old little girl is scheduled for surgery next week.

Nothing serious in the great big scheme of things. Except that she's my baby girl. An eye surgery that, ultimately, will accomplish the same thing as the ones I had 32 years ago did. But she's my baby girl.

It's outpatient - we'll come home later that day. But she's my baby girl.

Her surgeon is wonderful, herself an answered prayer. But this is my baby girl.

My son had the same surgery, at the same place, under the same capable hands of the same surgeon 6 years ago. I had a hard time then, too.

I know in my heart, and from my own experience, that her vision will be markedly better after the surgery. I know the risks of not proceeding with the surgery. Left untreated her vision issues may keep her from doing things that she wants to do later in life, and could lead to more serious issues down the road.

But it still hurts my heart thinking of her having to go through the surgery.

My son (who is 10 now) doesn't remember his surgery. She won't remember hers either. But I remember.

So today, while my kids were with their grandparents having a grand time, I was trying to accomplish about 5,000 things before things come to a screeching halt next week for a few days.

And occasionally I was crying.

I sent an email out this morning to several family members in other parts of the county, and to many friends, asking them to be in prayer for her, her surgeon, and us this coming week. Many people responded that they would indeed pray for all of us. As I was typing a response to my husband's cousin, also the mother of young girls, I found myself typing what I have said to many people, and thought to myself. "I'd do it myself for her if I could."

I hit "send" and then I heard a soft voice in my head.

"Suzanne, isn't that what I did for you?"

Wasn't expecting that.

But it is true.

What I wasn't able to do for myself, Christ did. He knew I needed something that I could not provide myself. Nothing I could do on my own would take away my guilt, my disobedience, and my hard-headed, stubborn, willful sins.

I couldn't pay that huge debt.

So He did it for me.

I would endure Elizabeth's coming post-operative discomfort for her if I could. He took unimaginable amounts of pain for me.

I would be the one who has to sit still for several days, being careful not to bump my eye, instead of her. He was nailed to a tree, unable to move, for me.

I would wear the bulky eye patch and the sticky surgical tape on my face for her. He wore a crown of thorns for me.

Why?

Because I love her. And He loves me.

He loves me.

The Creator and Sustainer of all loves me. **Me.**

And He loves my little girl. More than her Daddy and I do. More than humanly possible.

So, where does that leave me? I cannot take away the things headed her way, but I can place her in His hands. I can cover her, her surgeon, the operating room staff, the recovery room staff, all who are going to come in contact with her in prayer. I can rest knowing that even as much as I love my little ones, He loves them more.

And He is already there.

Lord, my faith is sometimes so weak. So small. Please be with my girl, with her surgeon, with the OR people, with the recovery room people, with everyone who will come in contact with her. Hold her, sustain her. Please send just the right people to minister to her. Lord, I pray for a speedy, quick recovery, with no problems. Go before her into the operating room and touch everything Lord.

Remove all germs, debris, anything that would cause harm. Lord post Your angels around her, around the doors, and protect all who are there. Lord, guide the surgeon's hands. And Lord, please come and be my Prince of Peace. I need Your peace and your comfort, Jesus. Amen.

"Immediately the boy's father exclaimed, 'I do believe; help me overcome my unbelief!'"
Mark 9:24

Pray Until They Get Here

"Rejoice always, pray continually, give thanks in all circumstances; for this is God's will for you in Christ Jesus."
1 Thessalonians 5:16-18 NIV

Sometimes I think I learn more from my children about how life should be lived than from anyone else. My son is driven to be the best at whatever he does. He does not tend to approach things he is going to do in a half-hearted manner. Full force, full on, gonna be the best.

My daughter is one of the happiest people I have ever run across. Always laughing, always smiling.

They both remind me in their own way of the joy in life. And often times of things I should be doing differently.

A year or so ago I wrote about my daughter praying to be a big sister.

She is at it again.

She has asked both her father and me "When can I have more brothers and sisters?" The last time she mentioned it to me I told her (again) that this was something she could talk to God about.

Her response to me was "Ok. I'll pray about it til they get here."

The simplicity of her response is beautiful.

And what she said holds so much!

She wants to be a big sister. So, she's going to pray about it. But that's not what stood out to me about what she said.

It's the expectation that is in her statement that stood out to me.

"Til they get here." Not "if" they get here. Not "I hope they get here." Her statement is full of the confidence that they **WILL** get here. She is fully confident that God will hear her request AND answer her.

That is an example I could stand to see over and over again.

There was no questioning in her prayer, no worries that God wouldn't hear, no worries that He wouldn't answer. Just confident assurance that He would handle it.

And then, just as she did the last time I wrote about her prayers, she gave it to God and went on about her business.

Hebrews 11:1 says: "Now faith is confidence in what we hope for and assurance about what we do not see."

I saw her faith in her words that day. Her childlike, wonderful, strong faith in her God. Confidence in what she hopes for.

Confidence in her God.

I pray that my faith will be as strong as the faith I saw in my daughter and that I will adopt that attitude of praying continually.

Thanks for the lesson, again, my little one!

Adopted

"God decided in advance to adopt us into His own family by bringing us to Himself through Jesus Christ. This is what He wanted to do, and it gave Him great pleasure."
Ephesians 1:5 NLT

Yesterday after lunch my little family of four headed to the hospital to visit a sick family member, Uncle Bill. (Names have been changed.) When we got there, we found that the particular ICU unit where he is being treated did not allow visitors under 18, and only allowed 2 visitors at a time. (I was glad that I had put some coloring books and crayons in my bag.)

My husband went in first.

While the kids and I were waiting (and coloring and reading comic strips on my phone) our pastor walked up. Soon after, hubby returned and our pastor and I went in to visit. During the time that we were in his room, the nurse came in. Uncle Bill introduced our pastor to his nurse, and then introduced me by saying "And this is my niece, Suzanne."

His introduction made me feel good. See, Uncle Bill is my uncle by marriage. Two marriages actually. Uncle Bill is the husband of my husband's mother's sister. So, we are not blood related. But that doesn't matter. Uncle Bill **_is_** my uncle.

Because both of my in-laws passed away before I met my husband, I have looked upon his aunts and uncles, particularly the three we see every Sunday at church, as my surrogate in-laws. Uncle Bill and his wife Aunt Mary are two of them.

They are good people. Easy to talk to. Easy to visit with. I enjoy their company, and feel in some way that I am knowing my husband's parents through them.

They have been accepting of me "into the family." It seems more natural for me to call them "Uncle Bill and Aunt Mary" than Mr. and Mrs. Miller. I am glad of that.

As I thought about our visit with Uncle Bill, I was reminded of the Scripture from Ephesians. The part that really stands out to me is the second part of that verse. "This is what He wanted to do, and it gave Him great pleasure." *It gave Him great pleasure*.

To me, it is amazing that adopting *me* into His family gave God, the Creator of everything, great pleasure. And to think that He decided "in advance" to accept me into His family. In advance of my birth, He knew I would disobey. He knew the sins I would commit and yet despite that, He chose to adopt me. And that gives Him great pleasure.

I find that so hard to wrap my brain around.

I have heard it said that adoption is when a child grows in your heart before you meet them. Years ago a friend of mine, who is herself adopted, and I were talking just a few months before my first born was born. She wasn't married at the time and said she wasn't sure if she would want to go through the whole long process of adoption if she was unable to have her own biological children.

I thought about that briefly and told her that I'm sure everyone is different but when I was ready to become a mother, I was SO ready. And I would have done whatever I needed to do to make that dream become a reality. Adoption included. (She, incidentally, is now the mother of a beautiful little boy.)

Isn't that what God did? Whatever was necessary to make it possible for humans to be with Him forever? Sending His Son to die in our place so that we could be with Him.

Romans 8:15 says that "Now we call him, 'Abba, Father.'" Abba being "Daddy," not just "father."

We are accepted, flaws and all, by God, if we but trust Him. We are part of the family.

And that gives us a home forever, and a forever home.

I am thankful for the family I didn't choose, and for the family that I did choose.

And I am thankful that God saw fit to extend His unfathomable love to us, His children.

Lord, help me to show family love to my brothers and sisters in You. Help me not to get caught up in "family squabbles" or "sibling rivalries." Thank you Lord for my family and keep Your hand on them. Amen.

Every Good and Perfect Gift

"Every good gift and every perfect gift is from above, and cometh down from the Father of lights, with whom is no variableness, neither shadow of turning."
James 1:17 KJV

Today is my son's birthday. My once chubby, happy baby is now a tall, lanky, happy 11-year-old.

I cannot believe he is 11. I'm sure next year I'll say "I can't believe he is 12." And one day "I can't believe he is 16!" and probably what will seem like the next week, "I can't believe my boy is 25!"

But it is true.

The time has gone quickly.

It seems like just yesterday that he was born.

After his birth, we sent out birth announcements to our friends and family. On them was a *really* adorable picture of him and the scripture from James 1:17a. I couldn't have picked a more appropriate scripture to describe my new baby. A good and perfect gift.

Not until he was born did I understand how my parents loved me. I knew they did, but becoming a parent myself gave me a new understanding.

Tonight as we drove home from my son's "pick the restaurant birthday meal," I commented to my husband on how much I love that child. And how it boggles my mind to think about what God did for us by sending His only Son to earth.

I have but one son. I cannot imagine sending him into a place where I knew he would be mocked, shunned, doubted, and ultimately beaten and killed. It goes against every parenting instinct I have to knowingly put my kids in danger. I want them protected and kept safe. I want them around people who will believe them and believe in them. I want my kids surrounded by people who will stick with them through thick and thin, through good and bad times.

Yet God sent His only Son to a place where He would be doubted. To people who would mock him. All but a few of

His friends deserted Him at what had to be the hardest time of His life.

Why did God do that?

Because of the rest of verse 17. The King James Version says it this way: "...the Father of lights, with whom is no variableness, neither shadow of turning."

God's character doesn't change. He doesn't even *hint* at changing. "Not a *shadow* of turning." He is holy.

We are not.

And because of that, there is a gap between us and Him. Only Christ could be the bridge to bring us back into a right relationship with God the Father. Only Christ. Nothing else. No amount of good that we do, no matter how much in our favor the balance sheet of "good done" versus "bad done" is, it's still not enough. Nothing.

God sent the most "good and perfect gift" ever when He sent Jesus to earth. The first step is for us to accept His gift.

And then let the Gift work in us every day to make us more and more like Him.

The perfect Gift.

Given to us.

Given for us.

The Gift that continues to give, every single day.

The Puppet Show

"My God sent His angel, and he shut the mouths of the lions. They have not hurt me, because I was found innocent in His sight. Nor have I ever done any wrong before you, Your Majesty."
Daniel 6:22 NIV

One day shortly after starting preschool, my four-year-old daughter was unloading her stash of papers from the day. She very excitedly pulled out three "puppets" that she had created during the day. Each puppet was a picture on a small square piece of paper, colored and attached to its own popsicle stick.

She excitedly told us that one was Daniel, one was the king and one was the "bad man." For the next 30 minutes or more she put on puppet show after puppet show behind my bed, telling the story of Daniel in the lion's den over and over. She was animated in her recounting of the events and took great pleasure in throwing the "bad man" into the lion's den at the end of each show.

Once she had tired of giving performances, she asked her father and me to take turns telling the story.

This is a story, having been raised in church, the daughter of a Baptist preacher, I have heard all my life. (Although not as many consecutive times as I had that day!) I am glad that my parents raised me in church, but I do think that sometimes I lose sight of just how miraculous many of the Biblical stories are since I have heard them for decades.

The story of Daniel and the lion's den is one such story. Retelling it myself to my four-year-old with her paper puppets, I thought of something I had never thought of before.

The lions were in the den the whole time Daniel was.

Of course they were, right? But it dawned on me that Daniel was in the den the whole night with the living, breathing, and no doubt, scary, lions.

They were not house cat type nice animals. They were vicious, strong killers. In fact, a few verses later the Scriptures tell us that the lions were so vicious that "before they reached the floor of the den, the lions overpowered hem and crushed all their bones." ("They" being the people thrown into the pit immediately after Daniel was pulled out.)

Crushed ALL their bones. Multiple people. All their bones. These were not docile animals Daniel spent the night with.

Daniel tells the king that the Lord sent "His angel" who shut the mouth of the lions" (v. 22).

The lions were kept from hurting Daniel, but Daniel was not lifted out of the pit until the next morning. So that means that he spent the whole night with the living, breathing, scary lions.

I guess on some level I knew that, but we read the story in such a few short verses that I never thought about the actual amount of time that elapsed between Daniel being tossed in, and being lifted out of the pit. Hours and hours.

God protected Daniel ALL NIGHT LONG. It wasn't a one-time event, but a continual event...all through the night the lions were kept from harming Daniel.

God didn't supernaturally lift Daniel from the den; He supernaturally delivered him *through* the den. He stayed with Daniel all night, keeping the danger at bay so that in the morning, not only was Daniel alive but "no wound was found on him" (v. 23).

I don't imagine the night passed quickly for Daniel. The lions didn't *poof* and disappear. They were there, big and powerful, all night. But the night *did* pass. And Daniel was safe through it all, protected in a way that only God could provide.

The message that jumped out to me through my experience in the four-year-old's theater? God will protect, continually. God will see us through the night, figuratively and literally. Even if we can still see the danger, God has it under control.

He can shut the mouths of lions.

He can keep people from even *smelling* like smoke after being in a fiery furnace.

He can raise the dead.

And He can certainly handle *all* of my problems.

After all, He used a four-year-old to show me something I should have seen long ago.

I thank you God that Your Word is alive and that You do still speak to us through it. Thank you for showing me something I had never noticed before. Please help me to trust You in all circumstances, lion or not. Amen.

My Daddy's Girl

"And I am convinced that nothing can ever separate us from God's love. Neither death nor life, neither angels nor demons, neither our fears for today nor our worries about tomorrow—not even the powers of hell can separate us from God's love."
Romans 8:38 NLT

As we rounded the corner in the driveway at our house Monday afternoon, we saw them.

Golf shoes and a box of apples on the side porch.

My daughter shrieked with excitement and began to holler "Daddy! Daddy!" See, this past weekend, my husband was out of town for his annual Man Trip to the Mountains. He and his buddies head to the mountains for some golf, hiking, and good food.

We stayed busy while he was gone, and he stayed in touch, but by Sunday our little girl was walking around saying "I want Daddy!"

When she realized he was home, she could not get out of the car fast enough.

In she went - straight into her Daddy's arms.

I know how she feels. I love my Daddy, too. As a child, Daddy was always able to calm my fears, make me laugh, say just the right thing. He still is.

One of the first times I went with my husband (before he was my husband) to his church, one of the older gentlemen in the church was called on to pray. Instead of opening his prayer with "Dear God," or "Our Father," he opened with "Daddy," and then began to address God. I had never, and still haven't, heard anyone else pray that way.

I have thought often about that gentleman's opening in his prayer.

I like it.

I've heard it said that it is not always a good thing when one is trying to share God with a nonbeliever to compare

God's love for us to a father's love for his children because there are those who haven't had a good earthly father.

I want to go on record as saying that my Daddy and my husband certainly do **not** fall into that category.

The characteristics I love and admire in my earthly father are evident in my heavenly Father as well.

Patience. Kindness. Self Sacrifice. Unconditional love.

How do I know that both my earthly and my heavenly Father have these traits? I have seen them exhibited over and over. I have tested them. And they have always proven that I can count on them.

I know that if I need him, my Daddy will be there, day or night. My Heavenly Father is there, all the time, everywhere. I know that I can trust my Daddy. He has never to my knowledge told me something that he didn't think was right. I believe that my Heavenly Father's Word is perfect and inerrant, in other words, *right*. Daddy was patient with me; as a child, in the teenage years, and even when I became an adult and frustrated him. The Lord has forgiven me again and again for the same things, again and again and again.

And he loves me.

And He loves me.

I once asked my Daddy if there was anything I could ever do to make him not love me. After he asked me what I was planning to do, he responded with "no."

I am glad I have that assurance. I knew it in my heart, but hearing it was nice, too.

And I am glad that I have the written assurance in my Father's Word, "*nothing* can ever separate us from God's love" (emphasis mine).

Thank you Daddy.

And thank You, Daddy.

Speaking Rocks

"I tell you," He replied, *"if they keep quiet, the stones will cry out."*
Luke 19:40 NIV

Recently my family and I took a mini-vacation to Virginia. They left me to plan the details, which meant there would be lots of stops at historical places...something I hope didn't get too old to them.

In between trips to various battlefields and monuments we stopped by The Grand Caverns in Grottoes. Five of the six of us went down into the caves to explore and take the tour.

To say it is a different world down there is an understatement. To say it is breathtaking would be another.

We started out on the surface and walked down, down, down until at one point we were 200 feet below ground. It was a bit chilly. Our guide had a flashlight, and there were dim lights throughout, lighting the trail. Good thing.

The trail leads through several "rooms" that are named...there is "the zoo" which features rock formations that look like a bison, a crocodile, an elephant and, of course, the zookeeper. There is the rainbow room, which has different colored lights illuminating the formations. There is Jackson's hall, named for General Stonewall Jackson, complete with a formation that looks like his horse, Little Sorrel. At the end of one long hallway is a formation called "George Washington." George doesn't look very big from a distance, but when you get close to him, you realize he is over 8 feet tall.

There are formations that are called "shields" and there is "cave sugar" which sparkles when you run your flashlight beam along it. There are formations made from countless years of running water that made the rocks look like jellyfish. And there are pools of water so still that even though they are only a few inches deep, they look to be too deep to step in.

Before we left the caverns, the guide turned all the lights out, including her flashlight. It was dark. Not dark like it is in our house at night, with the soft glow of the nightlight still lighting the hallway. Not even dark like it is outside our very rural, out-in-the-sticks house, where you can still see the stars and the light pollution from the nearest town.

Pitch. Black.

In the pitch blackness of the caves, it was impossible to see the wonders that surrounded us. But God can see them. God formed them. God formed them in the dark underground world. Psalm 139:12 says "even the darkness will not be dark to you." God creates in the dark.

And His work is beautiful.

All around us on that 90 minute trek underground was evidence of God's handiwork. His creation. It was He who directed the formations in the cave. It was He who directed the water where to flow to create the jellyfish-looking things. It was God who set things in motion to form the "Millennium Falcon" shield looooonnnnngggg before there was a Han Solo to fly the movie version.

We oftentimes see the beauty that God has created in the sky: rainbows, the stars, a beautiful sunset. Scripture mentions the beauty in the heavens. Psalm 19:1 reads "The heavens declare the glory of God; the skies proclaim the work of His hands." I was not expecting to be confronted with His marvelous handiwork underground. On that day I saw the work of His Hands declared *below* ground, in the beauty that was created in the darkness, far from any human intervention. As I walked past the "Rainbow Room" on the way out of the caverns I was reminded of what Christ said on His entry into Jerusalem when the people shouted praises to Him and the Pharisees told Jesus to quiet the crowd. Jesus's answer was: "I tell you," He replied, "if they keep quiet, the stones will cry out" (Luke 19:40).

I believe that on this particular day, I heard the stones shout praises to God in the depth and the dark.

I am thankful for the reminder of His work all around us...above, beside...and below.

Finger Painting

"...but your heavenly Father already knows all your needs."
Matthew 6:32b NLT

Every now and then my daughter decides she wants to paint. She alternates between painting at her brother's old easel and painting at the kitchen table. Lately, she has been painting at the table.

The other day was such a day. She was ready to paint the world's most beautiful mermaid.

She asked me if she could paint. I told her "yes" and no sooner (*literally no sooner*) had I gotten the words out of my mouth she started rattling off her list of needs. "Mommy, I need paint, and a brush and some paper and something to wipe my brush on..." and on and on she went.

Now, I have set up paint for her to finger-paint *hundreds* of times. Before her, I set up paint for her brother. I know how to set up the materials necessary for painting.

I said to her "Elizabeth, I know what you need...just be patient."

Then tap, tap, tap. I had a nudge in my heart.

How often do I do the same thing to Sovereign God? How often do I go on and on reciting by rote the things that I think I need, or the things I think I need Him to do. All without stopping, without really thinking about what I'm saying...just going over my "wish list."

Without really stopping to think that He already knows. It isn't necessary to go on and on.

He knows what I need *before* I ask. He knows my needs before I do.

And He knows the difference between my needs and my wants. I sometimes blur that line myself.

I do not mean to imply that God does not want to hear from us. Scriptures are quite clear that He does want to hear from us. He does want us to talk to him and share our thoughts, desires, fears, everything. It is also clear that we can (and should) keep asking for things that are important to us and praying for people who are important to us. Luke

9:9 says: "So I say to you, ask, and it will be given to you; seek, and you will find; knock, and it will be opened to you." But it isn't good to rotely, and without giving thought to my words, rattle it off without stopping to wait and hear from Him.

Stopping.

Waiting.

Listening.

These are all important parts of prayer that truthfully many times are missing from my prayer life. So often I am like Elizabeth was with her painting request...I go through my list of people to pray for, things to pray for, and "thank you for my blessings."

Then, too often, I'm done. I say my "amen" and get up to go about my business, crossing off "pray today" from my to-do list. When in reality, I'm missing the most important part. I'm not listening for God to speak to me. I'm not *getting quiet and being still.* I'm not being patient, as I often tell my children they should be.

My challenges to myself since God got my attention amidst the paintbrushes and Crayola paint are to start my prayers with thanksgiving, to really think about who and what I am praying for, and to spend some time being quiet before I say amen and move on.

And like I told my little mermaid artist, be patient.

The Cooper Filter

"Anger is cruel, and wrath is like a flood, but jealousy is even more dangerous."
Proverbs 27:4 NLT

From time to time I tell my husband that my "Cooper filter" has failed to kick in. "Cooper filter" being a reference to my grandmother, whose maiden name was Cooper, who had a colorful way of saying things. Ma, as we called her, was known for her way of, shall I say, speaking her mind. Often. She would share her opinion with you, even if you didn't ask. She was not one to shy away from letting her thoughts and opinions be known.

When I find myself speaking before I should, or speaking something out loud that really should have stayed in my head (and probably shouldn't have come into my head in the first place), I will say that my Cooper filter didn't work, i.e., it didn't "catch" the words on the way from my brain to my mouth. It let the words come out when they should have stayed in.

I had the opportunity just the other day to re-examine my filter. Apparently it either had a big hole in it, or it was clogged or something. The words came out when they most certainly should not have.

My sister-in-law and I had met for our girls to have a chance to play together. It was a nice day, especially for July in North Carolina. Low humidity and temps only in the high 80's, and the girls were having a grand time. My sister-in-law and I were trying to catch up on things, just chit-chatting. When she told me about a mutual acquaintance of ours who is pregnant. This person is married, has a house, already a mother, young, etc., etc. You would think my reaction would have been something like "Oh wow! That's great!" or "Fantastic! I hope she's doing well." Or even, "Wow! Wasn't expecting to hear that."

Nope.

My brain thought, and then my mouth uttered one word.

"WHY?!?!?!?"

My Cooper filter failed.

I dare say it was not the sound of happiness and joy for the expectant family.

Nope.

It dripped with something else.

And that was jealousy.

For years, we have wanted to have more children. Wanted and tried. Unsuccessfully. Several times we thought we were on our way, only to lose the baby.

So, honestly, from time to time, when I hear about other people's happiness in this area, I twinge with some jealousy. And I know it.

After I got home that day, I decided to look up jealousy in my Bible concordance. The verse from Proverbs jumped out and hit me upside my head.

The gist of it is that while anger and wrath are bad, jealousy is worse.

WORSE.

I thought about that. I have been super angry in the past (who hasn't) and I have felt like letting some red-headed wrath go on people from time to time. (I hope I'm not the only person who has had those thoughts.) And that wrath would not have been pretty. But to say that jealousy is worse?!?!? And not just worse, but dangerous.

What do we tell our kids about danger? Avoid it, right?

I have been studying on it and I think I have figured out why jealousy is worse and dangerous, at least for me.

Because it robs me of joy. It insists on focusing on what *isn't* here, instead of focusing on what *is* here. Yes, I want(ed) more children. But I don't need to let that fact interfere with the joy of the two I have. I don't need to focus on the ones that aren't here, but the ones who are. How can I teach my children to appreciate what they have been given, if I am not grateful and do not show appreciation for the gifts in my life?

That principle should apply to me not just about my children, but about life in general. I have been given so much, in non-material blessings and in material blessings. I should never ask for more. I have what I need, and more of what I want than I deserve.

And that is just earthly.

I have eternal life. Not because of anything I did, and certainly not because I deserve it.

Because He gave it to me. He has given me all that I have.

I should be sharing that, instead of allowing jealousy to creep up and take away my joy.

Plus, jealousy is not a shade of green that I look good in.

Better than ADT

"In peace I will lie down and sleep, for You alone, O Lord, will keep me safe."
Psalm 4:8 NLT

A few nights ago, my daughter and I had a girls' night out. It wasn't a girls' night I planned, it was because the men in our world had things going on that night. My tweenager was away for the weekend. My husband was playing golf with some friends. A night of golf for them always starts late in the afternoon so work won't be compromised too much, and ends with a meal out.

It's late when he gets home.

So, my daughter and I went to one of her favorite restaurants and then watched one of the movies she had recently checked out from the library. It was a sweet night.

At bedtime she brushed her teeth, said her prayers, and went on to bed. No problem.

I sat up for a while reading and waiting for Steve.

The quiet in the house is something I'm not used to. With two talkative children, there is usually someone having a conversation with someone else. Or by themselves.

It's never quiet.

It was nice for a little while.

Then, it was just weird.

I heard every creak the house made and every noise outside. I heard the cats scrambling around and occasionally hissing at each other. I heard dogs in the distance. I heard things I wasn't sure what they were.

The thought crossed my mind to try to go to sleep, but I didn't try.

Didn't think I could.

Not that I was scared. We live in a safe place. We have a dog that is big enough to scare someone if need be. He's pretty loud and has a big bark.

I'm just not used to going to sleep without Steve in the house.

When I lived by myself, it was no big deal. Come home, have some quiet time, grade some papers, watch some TV, eat supper, go to bed in the quiet. No problem.

That was my norm.

Now, it's not my norm.

My daughter went right to sleep without her daddy at home. She still felt just as safe and comfortable with me there as when Daddy is home. She knew that I was there to take care of her if she needed something.

The book of Psalms is one of my favorites in the Bible. There is a Psalm for *everything*. That is one thing I like about them. David wrote psalms of praise to God, but he also wrote psalms asking for peace and protection. He wrote psalms of confession and psalms that ask God to bring down judgment. (There is one verse in my translation that even says "slap all my enemies in the face!" Psalm 3:7 NLT)

In doing my Psalm Bible reading a few days after the girls' night I read Psalm 4. Verse 8 struck me. It tells me that I can rest easy, in peace, because God will keep me safe. "God alone" will keep me safe. I need nothing else, I need no one else. I like that in my translation "in peace" is first. The mental image that brings up is that I should already be at peace when I lie down to sleep. It's not "lie down and eventually sleep will take over." Or "lie down and keep worrying." It's "*in peace*, I can lay down and rest."

Now, I don't think that means that I should move to the worst part of town and leave my house unlocked when I sleep. What it does mean is that I shouldn't let things keep me up at night worrying. God will keep me safe. He can handle anything that I throw at Him, and anything that the world throws at me. I can rest knowing that He will keep me safe. That while things on earth may be dangerous, there are things that happen that are bad, there is nothing that can touch my eternal safety. That is secure. And I can rest knowing that.

God is enough to keep me safe, to keep me at peace, and to allow me to rest peacefully because He has it all in His hands. He has my earthly existence in His hands, but more importantly my eternal life is safe in His hands.

And that is better than any big barking dog or ADT sign.

Thankful for Tummy Trouble

"Now all glory to God, who is able, through His mighty power at work within us, to accomplish infinitely more than we might ask or think."
Ephesians 3:20 NLT

A few weeks ago my husband remarked to me how good he was feeling and how good he had felt for a while. He said "You know it's been two years since my attack."

I had not thought about that in a while.

He didn't lose his mind, go into some type of Hulk rage and attack someone. Nor did someone, or some wild animal, attack him.

Rather it was more of a health attack.

Steve had not been feeling well, didn't have much appetite, tired, just not himself. He made an appointment with his GP who told him that he was most likely dealing with acid reflux. She prescribed a medication for him. That was on a Friday.

Saturday morning he started the prescription. That night we went out to run some errands. We stopped to eat a quick supper. Steve didn't eat much. He didn't say much. He didn't look right.

I took the kids to church on Sunday. Steve still wasn't feeling well. We decided after I got home from church that we should go to Urgent Care. We got to the local Urgent Care who told us that they had a super long wait. They sent us to another Urgent Care, this one located at the hospital. There we were told pretty much the same thing, probably acid reflux, although they did mention gallbladder.

By this point, he was a little bit worried.

I was a little bit worried.

And still no improvement in how he was feeling, after more medication.

Truth be told, I was starting to imagine all sorts of unpleasant scenarios. Steve is a cancer survivor. I began to worry that it was back in some form and wreaking havoc on him. I began to worry some about his heart.

So, the mention of gallbladder was somewhat of a relief. I latched onto that and thought that was the best possible outcome of all the host of possibilities that could be wrong. In fact, I began to pray that it **was** his gallbladder. That can be fixed relatively easily I reasoned. A routine surgery, some recovery time at home, take it easy for a few weeks, then back to normal.

Monday came and went. No improvement.

Tuesday came. He was still not feeling well.

At all.

Steve decided he wanted to go to the ER. So after getting the kids to my parents, we took off to the ER.

And I got myself worked up into a *really* good worry-knot. Although I did try to hide it.

Our wait wasn't very long and we were taken back. In walks a young doctor, who made me feel old. He listened attentively, checked Steve out and gave him something he called a "GI cocktail." Within 5 minutes, Steve began to feel better. Much better. His color began to look normal again and he could feel real improvement.

When the doctor returned he diagnosed Steve's problem: gastritis.

Even more easily treated than a gallbladder.

So, two years later, after treatment and monitoring, Steve has had virtually no more problems like he did that week. (He did have an appointment with a cardiologist just to rule out any issues there...no problems.)

I thought about that week after Steve mentioned it to me the other day. I had worried and worried, all for what turned out to be something easily taken care of.

I had prayed for what I thought was the best solution. The best solution as I saw it.

But God had something else better. Something easier.

He handled the situation in a way that was easier than what I thought the easy way was.

How often in our lives does He do that for us? I think I see a way, but God says, "No...this way is best."

I think I know the answer but God says, "You don't quite have it there, Suzanne."

I think I know what's best, but God says, "Sit still. I've got something better!"

Ephesians says that God is able to accomplish "infinitely more than we might ask or think."

Infinitely more.

Think about that. Infinitely. Unending. Unending "more."
More, more, more, more than I ever thought possible.
More, more, more (and better, better, better) than I am
even capable of dreaming up.

The scripture says "more than we can ask" but it also says
"more than we can think." To me, that means that God has
things, blessings, planned for me beyond my wildest
dreams. Beyond my wildest imagination.

How often have I settled for something just because I
thought it was the best? When I didn't have the patience,
or the faith, to wait on Him?

He has the best for me. He sent His Best for me. I can
trust Him to show me what's best and to always have my
best interest in mind.

Not the Same

"For it is God who works in you to will and to act in order to fulfill His good purpose."
Philippians 2:13 NIV

During my recent "Tour of Local Homecoming Services," I had the chance to go to Homecoming at the church where my Dad currently serves as minister. The tradition at this church is to have a time of music prior to the regular service.

The music is always good. This year was no exception.

Usually, the music is provided by local groups, but generally they are folks I don't know. This year *was* an exception in that regard.

The music was provided by a local family...a dad, mom, and three girls. Each plays an instrument or two...or three. They all sing. They write some of their own music. They are really, really talented.

I went to high school, (and elementary school for that matter), with the father. And if you had told me in high school, or even a few years later, that I would be listening to him sing praises to God, and share the gospel, I would have thought you were nuts.

Completely.

He wasn't someone I thought had any knowledge of, or interest in, the Bible.

But there he was that Sunday morning laying things out for people. Straight. No frills, no mincing words, just the gospel, plain and simple. He talked about how he was not the same person he was before Jesus got hold of him.

He said something that I have heard said before; something to the effect of "God doesn't always call the qualified, but He always qualifies the called." Or put another way, He doesn't always call those we think are most equipped for His work, but He always equips those He does call.

I, for one, am thankful for all the examples in the Bible of people who perhaps don't fit our preconceived notion of someone that God would use. The Bible is full of them...

Abraham was impatient, took things into his own hands, and the result was all kinds of trouble for the nation of Israel for generations upon generations.

Jacob was a trickster.

Moses was, to start with at least, unwilling.

David was an adulterer. And a murderer.

Solomon, despite his wisdom, fell away from God.

And the women mentioned in Jesus's lineage? LOVE them!

Tamar wasn't married when she became pregnant.

Rahab was a prostitute.

Ruth was a foreigner.

Bathsheba was an adulteress.

Mary was young.

Over and over again we see people who may not have passed a seminary background check used in incredible ways. Those who haven't always lived as they should. The ones who didn't come from the right background, who didn't have the experience, or who just flat didn't fit the bill.

To us, anyway.

But to God, they were the right person for something. Something that was beyond our human eyes to see. But not beyond God's mind to dream up and see carried through.

During the message that the father of the band shared that Sunday, he called himself a "dumb chicken catcher." But he talked about God getting through to and using "this dumb chicken catcher" despite himself.

While I would argue that he is by NO means dumb, I do think he hit the nail on the head.

God can use us, despite ourselves, despite our past, and despite the baggage we may carry.

We just need to be open to Him.

Roots and Wings

"I pray that from His glorious, unlimited resources He will give you mighty inner strength through His Holy Spirit. And I pray that Christ will be more and more at home in your heart as you trust in Him. May your roots go down deep into the soil of God's marvelous love, and may you have the power to understand as all God's people should, how wide, how long, how high and how deep His love really is."
Ephesians 3:16-18 NLT

We made our annual trip to the photographer this past week to have our Christmas pictures taken. It is always a fun event for me. Plan the outfits, make sure we're all color coordinated, hair is in place, etc., etc. I'm always proud of the finished product.

This year was no exception.

The morning of the event, Jackson said to me, "Momma, I don't want to wear my glasses in the picture this year. I don't like the way they glare."

Which was fine with me.

Just as he said he was going to, when the photographer started shooting, he took his glasses off.

When we looked at the pictures, I couldn't help but notice how different he looked without his glasses. How grown up he looked.

I am not ready for that.

Wasn't he just born last week?

When we got home with the pictures, my husband began swapping out last year's pictures with the new ones from this year in our living room frames. As I looked at the old ones, I was struck again by how much my son has grown and changed in the last year.

Time goes by so quickly. I know I am going to blink my eyes and he is going to be headed off to college. With half my heart in tow.

My Daddy was fond of saying (when we were growing up) that he wanted to give my brother and me "roots and wings."

I now understand what he meant.

I want my little guy to soar. I want him to achieve what he can. I want him to use the intelligence that God has blessed him with for good.

But if he can do that from pretty close to me, that would be great too.

I want him to have deep roots too. I want him to have roots where we live. I don't think life gets much better than life in rural North Carolina. The people are kind, the land is beautiful, and the college sports rivalries are great! But that's not the most important type of roots I want him to have.

I want him to have roots like Paul talks about in his letter to the Ephesians. I want his roots to "go down deep into the soil of God's marvelous love." There is no richer soil. Just as soil provides all that a plant needs, I want God to be the place he (and his sister) go for all that they need. I want them to seek Him and His advice first, to let Him be the place they get their nourishment, to be what holds them in place.

To be what helps them grow tall and strong.

To be their anchor.

And never to forget, as this Scripture says, "How wide, how long, how high and how deep His love really is." That pretty much covers it all. Covers every place his wings could take him. Like the Psalmist says: "If I ride the wings of the morning, if I dwell by the farthest oceans, even there Your hand will guide me, and Your strength will support me" (Psalm 139:9-10).

I want him to remember that as much as his mother loves him, His Heavenly Father loves him more.

And that everywhere he goes, that love will follow him, lead him and hold him.

I know if he keeps his roots deep in God's soil, he will go far.

And I hope those wings will bring him home to his Momma from time to time.

Floor Sleeping

"As a mother comforts her child, so will I comfort you: and you will be comforted over Jerusalem."
Isaiah 66:13 NIV

I am sure there are some who would say my husband and I are warping our daughter for life.

She has been sleeping on the floor in our room for about a month now. Her choice. She has a room of her own, with a nice, big double bed. She has a set of Minnie Mouse sheets on her bed, complete with a nice big Minnie Mouse comforter. She has a plethora of stuffed animals to pile around her in the bed.

But she wants to be on our floor.

So, every night, I make a pallet on the floor of many blankets topped with a sheet and her pillows. Throw in 7 or 8 of her special friends, her brother's "Froggy banklet" that she confiscated, another sheet to cover up with, another heavy blanket and she is good to go.

Most nights before bedtime her Daddy asks her "Where are you going to sleep tonight?" To which she giggles and tells him "your room" with a laugh, as if to say "Why do you even need to ask, Daddy?"

I am not quite sure why she wants to sleep in our room, but I think I have a pretty good idea.

She likes us.

We make her feel safe and secure.

If she should need something, she needs only to call "Mommy!" or "Daddy!" and we are right there. (Although sometimes I must admit when she calls me in the middle of the night, I am less than enthusiastic about helping.)

Even though I am not always the most excited about locating a lost animal or the missing covers in the middle of the night, I think that I am pretty good at being comforting when the kiddos are sick.

Even now as a 40+ year-old adult, when I don't feel good, I wouldn't mind my Momma showing up to sit with me, bringing me a cool cloth or just being in the room with me. My Momma is the best at being Nurse Mommy. Just the "Momma presence" makes me feel better.

Why?

I think it is the unconditional love. My Momma loves me. I love my babies. Unconditionally. Wholeheartedly. With every fiber of my being. I know it. They know it. I know that my Momma will do whatever she can to make me feel better when I am not well, just as I would do the same for my two.

I have my limitations though. I am, after all, only human.

But God knows no limits.

He is not bound by human knowledge or physical limitations.

He is capable of everything.

And He loves in a way that we cannot comprehend.

He promises to comfort us as a mother comforts her children. But since He is capable of so much more than we are as mere humans, His love and comfort are exponentially more than what we can offer.

I don't think I claim that promise as much as I should.

I do reach for Him when things aren't so great, but I don't always spend as much time with Him, "recharging" as I should when things are good. He promises to comfort us, to love us and to never leave us. His promises are always kept.

And, unlike me, He is never asleep in the middle of the night if I call Him. He knows where *my* blanket is. He is never half asleep filling my needs.

If the Greeter Only Knew

"They will be divided, father against son and son against father, mother against daughter and daughter against mother, mother-in-law against daughter-in-law and daughter-in-law against mother-in-law."
Luke 12:53 NIV

Recently after completing a "haven't you been to the grocery store in a month" huge shopping trip I ran into a lady that I have not seen for a long time. Right at the entrance/exit of the particular store. Right near the greeter.

This lady has lived an interesting life and is very easy to talk to. In fact, one can pretty much not say anything and the conversation will continue.

Having not seen her in some time, there was much catching up to do.

Simple pleasantries were exchanged...how are the kids, how are your folks, how is the job, etc., etc.

It didn't go beyond that though.

Good thing.

Because had it gone much deeper than surface pleasantries we could have had deep unpleasantries.

And I don't think the door greeter who was watching us would have smiled on that.

While this is a nice enough person and she is easy to talk to, she and I could not be any more different on most levels. Politically, on social issues, economic theory, preference on places to live, I could go on and on.

I am not sure she knows how different we are. While she is open and eager (*very eager*) to share her world view on almost any topic, I am not. (Yet another difference.) I generally do not approach the tinderbox topics that can lead to confrontations, especially not in public places. And since I won't see her again (probably) anytime in the near future, what is the point in opening a can of worms?

Later, I processed some of the things she had said, and some of the things that implied, if not directly stated, her particular worldview.

I don't know her religious views. I know how she was raised but I don't know if she continues to practice her childhood faith, or any faith at all.

I came across the verse from Luke not too long after running into her. And I thought of her.

We (she and I) are divided on all the BIG issues of the day. And there is the possibility that we are divided on religious beliefs as well. And while that is sad, it doesn't affect my day to day life. She's not part of my day to day life. How sad I would be if my mother and I were divided on our beliefs, or my daughter and I in our beliefs, as are the people in Luke 12:53.

I have always interpreted this verse to be a warning of the end times and how people who should be united will be divided in their beliefs about things of the physical world and, more sadly, of the spiritual world. Divided because one will follow Christ, and the other will not. That kind of separation would be very tough, I think.

To my knowledge, I've never lost a friend because I am a Christian. Most everyone in my family shares my beliefs. I live in the "Bible Belt" and while things are certainly different here than they were when I was a child, people, for the most part, are not ostracized for being Christian.

But I fear that the day is coming. I fear my children will face things I didn't have to. I am concerned about the kind of place this world will be when I am a grandmother.

Christ's warning in Luke 12 is a stern reminder to me that I need to be diligent in my prayers for my family (especially my children) and my friends (including my children's friends). Diligent in asking God to strengthen their faith, and to give them discernment against the teachings of false doctrine, strength to stand their ground for Christ when they are challenged, and the words to say to someone who would need to hear the Truth.

And I hope that my friends and family are diligent in their prayers of that nature for me. I need them, too.

God's Timing

"To everything there is a season, and a time to every purpose under the heaven."
Ecclesiastes 3:1 KJV

A couple of months ago my friend Janet texted me and said she was cleaning out her sewing stuff and if I wanted some of it to let her know. Seeing as how I am attempting to relearn how to sew, I jumped at the chance. (You never need an excuse to go out to supper with one of your best buds either, but this was a solid excuse!)

Janet had a plethora of stuff to give me...much of which I had to ask "What is *this*?" and "What do you do with *that*?" She also told me that she would soon have bunches of quilting fabric to get rid of and wanted to know if my Aunt Mary Lea would like it. Aunt Mary Lea is a quilter and she

113

and Janet have often talked at family functions about their mutual love of quilting.

Sure enough it wasn't too much longer before Janet called to tell me she had the fabric ready to send on.

After we met and I got the fabric, I called my aunt and told her what I had for her. She said she would in fact love to look through the fabric and would be more than happy to share with the other ladies in her quilting circle. I texted Janet later to tell her that Aunt Mary Lea would use it and to ask her if I had her permission to take the rest to the new local hospice house. Some ladies in the community are making blankets for each person who comes through and are taking donations of fabric.

Janet's text back to me caught me off guard. It said "I would absolutely LOVE it if you would take it to the hospice house. Hospice in Martin County was a Godsend when Momma was sick. And this is perfect timing as tomorrow will be 15 years since Momma's passing."

After reading her text, I thought to myself "That has got to be God's timing."

I believe God has a purpose to everything and that He is in control of all events. But sometimes the little reminders that I don't expect startle me.

or all of the things to happen in the right order and in the ight time for us to be having that conversation when we id could not be coincidence, in my opinion.

think God uses things like this to remind me that He is in ontrol. And that He does have a plan. And to remind me hat He is working all the time to bring about good things. I nay not always see what He's doing and I am often times often times!) unaware of His hand moving, but His hand is noving nonetheless. I may not understand what He is loing, or the timing in which He operates but I don't have o understand. I just need to trust and know that He will vork all things out in His timing.

Recently I have begun reading a book by Lysa TerKeurst for Sunday School unit I am co-leading. There are a couple of quotes from the book that really stuck out to me and are pplicable in all of life, and especially true when thinking of God's timing. (I wish I could take credit for coming up with hese, but I can't.) One is "Can I trust God to be God?" and he other is "God is good at being God." I have to trust that God has *everything* under His control, including the timing of things. He knows just the right time for things to happen nd in just the right ways they should happen.

My job is to be ready.

And maybe being ready will help me not be surprised the next time He shows me He has it all worked out.

A Sparrow and a Dog

"Are not two sparrows sold for a penny? Yet not one of them will fall to the ground outside your Father's care. And even the very hairs of your head are all numbered. So don't be afraid; you are worth more than many sparrows."
Matthew 10:29-31 NIV

Yesterday was a little bit stressful.

My oldest had to return to the dentist for a filling, something he has never experienced before. But that was not the part that really had me worried.

I had to take his little sister with us because our child care plans changed at the last minute. Keeping her occupied in the same room her brother was having his tooth worked on was a bit of a concern for me, but that wasn't what really ad me worried. (Incidentally, she did very well with her oloring books to keep her entertained.)

One of our dogs was sick. That was what had me worried.

This is the first dog my son has ever owned. The dog lives with my Momma and Daddy but he is still "our" dog. He was a gift to my son when he was about 3 from my friends Doug and Lynda. Jackson named him "Hunley" after the obby dog on the Curious George shows...which was a favorite of his at the time.

Hunley is enormous...a huge chocolate lab with the most soulful brown eyes. And he is as sweet as he can be. When we are at my folks' house, he is right there with us. Always wanting to be with us. In fact, he made the family portrait this past year on Mother's Day. There has never been a sweeter dog.

So, having him sick was worrying me a little. Especially because we thought it was something big and bad. He wasn't eating; he was drooling and looking funny around the mouth.

When Momma called to tell me she was taking him to the vet, I sent a text to my friend Janet telling her that Hunley was sick and to say a prayer for him. Then I thought to myself "That was silly...he's a dog...there are other things to be praying for." I prayed for him anyway. A bunch.

But the more I have thought about that, I have come to the conclusion that my thought process was flawed. In fact, I think it was downright incorrect.

Wrong for a couple of reasons.

One, I think, is that God does want to hear from us. He wants us to talk to him about what is going on in our lives, even though He already knows. Just like I want my kids to talk to me about things they are doing, even when I know full well, I still want to hear from them. I want to interact with them. It makes me happy. God created us to have a relationship with Him. Talking to Him is one way to maintain and strengthen that relationship.

My dogs are important to me. When something matters to me, it matters to God. He loves me. Why would He not be interested in the things that concern me?

The other thing is that dogs are part of His creation. They are part of the world He made. Genesis tells me that after God created His world, He looked at it and pronounced that it was good. It was good, including the creatures He made. And that includes dogs. (Personally I think He may have looked at the dogs He created and thought "*That* is a *very good* creation!")

God cares about His creation and His creatures in creation. He is aware of them and their needs just as He is aware of me and my needs. The verses I quoted from Matthew show that. Even though these verses don't deal directly with Creation, they are proof to me that God cares about it. Jesus tells His disciples that not one sparrow will fall to the ground without God being aware of it. The verse goes on to tell us that we are more valuable to Him than sparrows, but He is certainly aware of all creation.

Including my brown dog.

So, while I think it is evident in Scripture that we are way more valuable to Him than the other creatures He made, I think they are important to Him as well. He cares for them. And He cares that I care about my dogs. He knows that I love them and He knows how important they are to me.

Later in the day I got a call from Momma saying the vet had worked her magic and that after some TLC, a shot for pain and swelling, Hunley was going to be fine. He came home with some medicine and was feeling much better.

I'm glad.

Really, really glad.

The verses in Matthew tell me that the very hairs of my head are numbered. I believe the Lord in heaven knows the same about Hunley.

And loves every single brown hair!

Mercy

"When the accusers heard this, they slipped away one by one, beginning with the oldest, until only Jesus was left in the middle of the crowd with the woman."
John 8:9 NLT

The book of John is one of my favorite ones in the Bible. I like the way John writes. He gives details, and is a little wordier than others. My husband has told me it is because I am a "word" person, much more so than he is.

So after finishing up my Bible reading plan from the past two years, and much mental debate, I decided to start with re-reading John to go along with my daily Psalm. One chapter per day.

Today being January 8, I read John chapter 8.

n it is the story of the woman caught in the act of adultery
nd the efforts of those in the community to stone her.

gain today, the Holy Spirit showed me something I had
ever noticed.

his woman was obviously guilty of sin. Caught in the very
ct. Possibly facing death. Until Jesus intervened.

ut that isn't what stood out to me today.

t was a combination of verses 7 and 9. In verse 7 we see
esus saying in response to the calls to stone her "All right,
ut let the one who has never sinned throw the first stone!"
NLT). In verse 9 we see that everyone is gone. Everyone
xcept Jesus. Everyone except "**the one who has never
inned**" (emphasis mine).

never caught that before.

LL were gone. Without their rocks, without another word
at least none recorded in Scripture), without throwing the
irst pebble. All except Christ. The only **One** who never
inned (emphasis mine).

Vhat that said to me was He is the only one with the real
uthority to condemn me. The only One with the right to
throw the stone." Why? Because He is without sin.

It was His law that she had broken. And His laws that I break.

Daily.

But what was His response? Did He say "Ok, now watch out woman! Here come the rocks!"? Did He call down boulders to fall from the sky and crush her for her sins?

No.

He stands and speaks to her.

He doesn't accuse. He doesn't condemn. He doesn't scold, fuss, or even tell her that she has been bad. (I'm pretty sure she was aware of that anyway.)

He simply tells her "Neither do I (condemn you). Go and sin no more."

If that is not a picture of mercy, I don't know what is.

Christ, the One without sin, the One who created the universe, the One who rightly could have judged and punished her, didn't.

He offered her a second chance.

ot a second chance to "go and sin again, and this time be more careful. Don't get caught." No, a second chance to Go, and **sin no more**."

esus knew that she was human. As am I. That it was mpossible for her to never sin again. It is impossible for me not to sin.

But I should try. I should try to do better. I should make he effort to end bad habits and try to sin no more.

And I should be grateful to Him that He neither threw His ock, nor simply dropped it and walked away.

He never picked one up.

Family Thanksgiving

"And the angel said to me, 'Write this: Blessed are those who are invited to the wedding feast of the Lamb.' And he added, 'These are true words that come from God.'"
Revelation 19:9 NLT

Thanksgiving has always been one of my favorite holidays. It was always the time when my Daddy's side of the family gathered from various places in the United States and abroad to be together.

This year was one of the biggest we have had. This was partly due to the fact that the next generation is increasing in number and the fact that we had some friends there this year as well. My Alabama cousin and her family weren't there due to a recent oral surgery, and my brother and his family weren't there due to a brand new baby and a sick lder child, but other than that, everyone who should have been there was. We did, at least briefly, get to see my brother when we took the young ones over to his house to see Pork Chop the pig.

We had a huge lunch complete with turkey, dressing, potatoes and way more dessert than was needed.

Generally not too long after everyone gets there something is said in reference to my grandparents. They were all one-of-a-kind, each in their own way. And while they were here on earth and able, they ate with us; Momma's parents, and Daddy's parents. Remembering them always makes me/us smile. Those were good times.

As we sat around and visited and watched the next generation begin to make memories that hopefully they will look back on one day and cherish, I thought about how all of us there are different. We grew up in different parts of the country, with different friends, were involved in different activities, most went to different colleges, and for the most part have different careers. Among those gathered we have psychologists, a surgeon, two ministers, a couple of teachers, an actress, various types of designers and some stay-at-home mothers. We have Democrats, Republicans, and "unaffiliateds." We have UNC fans, and we have NCSU fans. We have big talkers and we have big listeners.

But we are family.

As I thought about how we are all different, I thought also about the one thing that binds us together...our shared heritage and our shared memories. We gathered around (several) tables to celebrate that.

And I thought about how one day, unless Jesus returns in our lifetime, all of us will be a memory to someone. I hope a pleasant memory.

But that doesn't mean that the feasting and the gathering o family will stop.

We are assured in the Scriptures that those saved by the grace of Jesus will gather together to celebrate again. This time at a heavenly banquet. A banquet put together by the Lord himself for those who are called by His name.

There will be no missing those who have gone on before us because they will be there! I can only imagine what joy that will be. I would love to be able to have a meal again with all of my grandparents, aunts, uncles, cousins and friends who were once here. And also to be eat with the people we read about in the Bible.

And that won't even compare to being with Jesus himself, the One who is the Bread of Life to us.

The things that make us different on Earth won't matter anymore. ALL there will be His children. The book of Matthew (chapter 8, verse 11) tells us that the feast will be inclusive of all who have called on His name: "And I tell you this, that many Gentiles will come from all over the world—from east and west—and sit down with Abraham, Isaac, and Jacob at the feast in the Kingdom of Heaven."

We will be made perfect, in perfect bodies to enjoy the perfect harmony of being with the Perfect One.

We will feast and rejoice in a way unknown here on Earth.

That is something to be thankful for this Thanksgiving season (and all the time!).

Amen and pass the potatoes.

Tweakings and Tappings

Comments? Questions?

I would love to hear from you.

Please email me at:

TweakingsAndTappings2@gmail.com

If you enjoyed this book, please consider leaving a review at www.amazon.com.

Made in the USA
Columbia, SC
04 August 2019